THE GENRE WRITER'S BOOK OF WRITING PROMPTS & STORY IDEAS II

Copyright © 2023 by the Mayday Writing Collective

ISBN 979-8-3949359-2-3

Printed in the United States of America

10 9 8 7 6 5 4 3 2 1

The Genre Writer's Book of Writing Prompts & Story Ideas II

540 MORE Creative Writing Prompts in the Genres of Fantasy, Sci-Fi, Mystery & Thriller, Horror & Supernatural, and Romance

Created and compiled by the Mayday Writing Collective

INTRODUCTION

Since the Mayday writing team released *The Genre Writer's Book of Writing Prompts & Story Ideas*, we've heard from hundreds of writers who've used our prompts and ideas to get back into writing, craft stories, run tabletop role-playing games, publish their first novel, and even kick-off their self-publishing careers. Wow! We couldn't be more proud of each and every one of you and we're honored that our little book was able to inspire you.

Now the Mayday writing team is back with 540 MORE prompts and story ideas. As we said before, there are days when the words come easily and days when they don't—and sometimes days when no words come at all. And we're here once again to help you keep things moving when writer's block simply won't get off your coach, pack its bags, and say goodbye.

We remain a tight-knit team of genre writers, now with two new faces in the mix, and we're inching up on having published three hundred books in total. We want to offer you our combined knowledge and experience in the form of our writing prompts and story ideas so you can kick your writer's block to the curb and do what you love doing most: creating amazing tales that delight and surprise.

We've put together another 540 prompts—108 prompts in five genres—that represent long months of brainstorming sessions and hours of creative discussion among our writers. Why 108? Is it because of the number's significance in Hinduism and Buddhism? Or its appearance in martial arts? A secret connection to the number of cards in a deck of UNO?

Truth be told, we were (and still are!) just drawn to it. We hope you find it as enchanting a number as we do.

We'd love to see what stories you spin from the prompts in this book. Share them with the world by using the hashtag **#writingmayday** on your social network of choice.

Happy writing!

USING THIS BOOK

You're welcome to use this book any way you see fit, but the Mayday writing team has a few suggestions to help you get the most of out of all 540 writing prompts:

The Random Roll. This is our favorite way to pick a prompt. Go to a random number site such as random.org (or roll some dice!) and generate two random numbers, one between 1 and 5 and another between 1 and 108. The first number is the genre to write in—Fantasy (1), Sci-Fi (2), Mystery & Thriller (3), Horror & Supernatural (4), Memoir (5)—and the second is the prompt in that genre. If you want to restrict yourself to a specific genre, just leave off the first roll. As you work through prompts, mark off their stamps to keep track of which ones you've completed.

Once you have your prompt, you need to set how long you'll be writing for. This is where our signature **90-7-30 system** comes in. Here's how it works:

If you're a beginning writer or you're short on time, start with **90 seconds** of nonstop writing per prompt. This easy-to-achieve time limit lets you stretch your writing muscles on a regular basis, and the nonstop requirement keeps your mind from wandering.

If you're ready for something more, it's time to move on to **7 minutes** per prompt. You should still aim to write as continuously as possible during these minutes, but you should also seek to produce a cohesive passage, with a clear beginning and middle (and end, if you can fit it in there).

When you're feeling limbered up, go ahead and try for a whopping **30 minutes** of writing. It's likely you'll have a few pauses here and there, and that's okay—the focus of the 30 minute writing block is dedication and discipline. Stay put for the entire duration (if life allows) and make sure you avoid checking email, Facebook, Instagram, Tik Tok, or any of the other million distractions that are trying to keep you from writing.

You can even revisit each prompt with different 90-7-30 time limits, exploring old ideas or giving life to new ones. Be creative, be daring, be you!

Keep your writing organized. It helps to have one place where you do all of your writing so that you can refer to it any time you want. Maybe that's a notebook, a computer document, or even the notes app on your phone. Our personal favorite are Rollbahn's spiral-bound notebooks for physical writing and the ultra-convenient Google Docs for digital work.

Set a goal. You don't have to write everyday (though we recommend it!) but you should commit to writing a set number of times a week and sticking to it. It will be hard at first, but writing is like every other skill—you need regular practice for it to improve. And if you decide on 90 seconds of writing per prompt, that's less than 5 minutes a week. You can spare that, right?

The more you write, the better you'll get. Take it from us and the collective ten of thousands of pages we've written. You can do this.

FANTASY WRITING PROMPTS

"Fantasy isn't just a jolly escape: It's an escape, but into something far more extreme than reality, or normality. It's where things are more beautiful and more wondrous and more terrifying. You move into a world of conflicting extremes."

Terry Gilliam

1. A charismatic cult leader claims to be the reincarnation of an ancient Death god who is trying to amass followers to summon the undead.

_____

_____

_____

_____

_____

2. After the rains fell, the city twisted itself into a new shape.

_____

_____

_____

_____

_____

3. Before Krella would look into the silver pool, she made a promise: she would only share what she herself could not bear alone.

_____

_____

_____

_____

_____

4. Never underestimate the usefulness of a hungry dragon.

_____

_____

_____

_____

_____

5. Blood magic was the only magic King Yxyowl could not abide, because he was determined to keep its dark power for himself.

_____
_____
_____
_____
_____

6. When mythological creatures suddenly appear in modern-day cities around the world, humanity must adapt to living alongside gods and monsters from ancient legends or risk being destroyed by them.

_____
_____
_____
_____
_____

7. The mysterious artifact known as the Dreamstone is said to grant its possessor control over their dreams—and a way for their nightmares to enter the waking world.

_____
_____
_____
_____
_____

8. It was supposed to be just another day at Wizdross Academy until the Witcheater arrived.

_____
_____
_____
_____
_____

9. In the bustling city of Plestra, magic is outlawed. When aspiring mage Horos stumbles upon a network of secret spellcasters though, he realizes the ban on magic is not what it seems.

_____
_____
_____
_____
_____

10. It was said that no one could enter or leave Lake Mirra without passing through its guardian, a seven-armed octopus desperate for its missing limb.

_____
_____
_____
_____
_____

1. The moment she played the first note on her enchanted harp, the earth beneath her began to tremble.

_____
_____
_____
_____
_____

2. A young healer with the ability to mend wounds by absorbing them into her own body is captured to save the life of a vicious dictator and must choose between saving her own life or letting the dictator perish.

_____
_____
_____
_____
_____

13. An odd traveler arrives in town, offering to grant one wish to each resident in exchange for a single memory. But this traveler seems to want these memories for nefarious reasons.

_____
_____
_____
_____
_____

14. Scattered throughout the Northern Lands are seven sacred instruments. Played together, they can destroy the world—or remake it.

_____
_____
_____
_____
_____

15. A powerful wizard becomes disillusioned with the power of his magic and seeks a worthy successor, who in return for these magic powers will never be able to sleep. But there's a catch: the successor must be a newborn baby.

_____
_____
_____
_____
_____

16. When soulmates are born, they share a unique birthmark that only becomes visible when they come into close proximity with each other.

_____
_____
_____
_____
_____

17. Wisteria is a world where everyone is born with magic coursing through their veins... until a baby is born with no magic, only the ability to nullify the magic of others around them.

_____

_____

_____

_____

_____

18. In Josie's backyard, the portal opened again. Again, she saw herself standing there, but this time she wore a crown of fire.

_____

_____

_____

_____

_____

19. The world had always been alive with magic, but now it seemed to be rotting from the inside out.

_____

_____

_____

_____

_____

20. In a city ruled by fantasy beings, humans are forced into servitude and treated as lesser beings. One human resistance fighter infiltrates the ruling council, determined to overthrow their oppressors and bring equality back to their world.

_____

_____

_____

_____

_____

21. At the end of the Dwarven invasion of an Elvish woodland stronghold, both sides realize they are being manipulated by humans to fight one another.

_____

_____

_____

_____

_____

22. Three noble Orc princes compete for the hand of the widowed Elven queen, not knowing that the queen is in love with their sister.

_____

_____

_____

_____

_____

23. When the lonely witch Cassina discovers an abandoned baby in the woods with dangerous magical abilities, she must decide whether to raise the baby as her own or leave it in the woods.

_____

_____

_____

_____

_____

24. Long ago, great glowing lights called "stars" dotted the night sky. Now, with a precious so-called star seed in his possession, Drazel will attempt to light the night sky up again before his city is besieged by creatures from the dark.

_____

_____

_____

_____

_____

25. Djrei crept into the great hall in the dead of night and sat upon his brother's throne. It would soon be his—if the dragon-faced centipede was to be believed.

---

26. You never bought from Mapmaker Zol, not without warding the maps first. How do you think he got into all those people's houses anyway?

---

27. The best thieves were the ones no one knew. And absolutely everyone knew Calendine.

---

28. The darkness of the underground yawned wide, as black as the dead eyes of the Spider King. Even though it was forbidden, Shale wished he'd brought a torch.

---

29. Kayla had never held a Moonbloom before, but as it opened under the new moon sky, she realized she'd made a terrible mistake.

_____
_____
_____
_____

30. Blades, guns, bladeguns, Nils had seen it all. That was why he'd studied magic, he thought as he threw his spell dice into the crowd of ravenous orcs. It was much more reliable. The dice landed with a burst of light, transforming into a broken sword and an unloaded pistol. "Not again," groaned Nils.

_____
_____
_____
_____

31. Grael had always wanted to travel to the Lands Below. But first he neede a willing host body, should the rumors be true.

_____
_____
_____
_____
_____

32. After a startling solar flare, pets all across the globe begin speaking to their owners in their native tongues.

_____
_____
_____
_____

33. Sir Retogahl sloughed off his armor and looked down at the wound in his gut. He had to give the gem to someone else before it was too late.

_____
_____
_____
_____
_____

34. The only time that anyone ever took a skiff out into the Swamp Sea was for coin or bloodshed. In my case, thanks to my lying, two-faced brother, it was both.

_____
_____
_____
_____
_____

35. Revenge was the only thing on Dashoke's mind. Revenge for the guard commander who'd brought him, revenge for the wizard who'd framed him, and revenge for the executioner who had killed him.

_____
_____
_____
_____
_____

36. A teenage girl's writing starts coming to life, allowing her to summon fantastic creations—until they begin to demand to return to their world of words.

_____
_____
_____
_____

37. As I stood atop the desolate hill, overlooking the once-thriving city now lost beneath ravenous vines and twisted roots, I knew our time had come.

_____

_____

_____

_____

_____

38. Oh, sure, everyone's up for an adventure when it's to the Warm Woods the Graceful Gardens, but suggest one tiny visit to the Skull Sea and all of a sudden you're all alone at the tavern. Well, just more treasure for, I suppose

_____

_____

_____

_____

_____

39. Deep within the Crystal Caverns lies an enchanted pool that can alter one's appearance at will. But there's a price: Once changed, someone else i the world will be forced to take on the user's old appearance.

_____

_____

_____

_____

_____

40. As she gazed up at the colossal, crystal Aph tree, she wondered how something so beautiful could also be the world's greatest threat.

_____

_____

_____

_____

_____

41. Each year, the spirits of the harvest arrive bringing great bounties to last the plainsfolk through the long winter. When they don't show up one year, the plainsfolk start pointing fingers to figure out who wronged the spirits.

_____

_____

_____

_____

_____

42. In a secluded castle shrouded in mystery, residents pay tribute to their enigmatic ruler through elaborate masquerade balls that involve inviting unsuspecting outsiders.

_____

_____

_____

_____

_____

43. Everyone was looking for pieces of the broken sword, sure it would be the people's' salvation. But no one thought to look for the shield that broke it.

_____

_____

_____

_____

_____

44. The mining operation in the wastelands had gone awry, leaving not a single dwarf, goblin, or gnome alive.

_____

_____

_____

_____

_____

45. The obsidian collar protects its wearer from even the most deadly fires, as long as they remember that they can never, ever get it wet.

_____

_____

_____

_____

_____

46. The Goblin King, who has kept peace with the Dwarven Alliance for more than a hundred years, has died. Now it's time for a successor, which will cause his dwarf-loving son to clash with his warmongering daughter.

_____

_____

_____

_____

_____

47. The blacksmith Tunyas can imbue metal with the blood of monsters to make his weapons more deadly. But when the Galath the Monster Lord kidnaps Tunyas, he'll be forced to make weapons against humankind.

_____

_____

_____

_____

_____

48. The Great Library of Archaius contains knowledge from across dimensions and timelines. But with no way to sift through the Library's contents, its visitors are left to wander the vast halls hoping they can find what they need.

_____

_____

_____

_____

_____

49. When Querra saw the gravel on the open windowsill, she knew someone had been feeding the gargoyles again.

_____

_____

_____

_____

_____

50. A humble baker discovers they possess the power to bring their tasty creations to life, using them to stage an uprising against a corrupt tyrant king.

_____

_____

_____

_____

_____

51. Trolls. Those were the real problem on the Gaunt Plain. They were tall, never slept, and always hungry. Not to mention how they liked their meat: fresh.

_____

_____

_____

_____

_____

52. The legends spoke of Azkathar as the most terrible dragon to ever sail through the skies. But to the Lilliputians who lived upon his back, he was their savior.

_____

_____

_____

_____

_____

53. In Bredell, emotions can be harnessed as powerful energy sources. When the empath Yule discovers he can manipulate emotions, he's pulled into a far-reaching conspiracy.

_____

_____

_____

_____

_____

54. A reclusive inventor creates a sentient clockwork automaton that captures the hearts and imaginations of all who meet it, but what will happen when its creator dies, leaving its future uncertain?

_____

_____

_____

_____

_____

55. Khreshlyn had sailed the seas, the skies, the deserts, and even the icy plains. But sailing time? Only a fool would mess with that kind of magic, he say. I guess in Kreshlyn's eyes that made me the biggest fool of all.

_____

_____

_____

_____

_____

56. The best potion masters never taught their secrets, knowing how much that would hurt their sales.

_____

_____

_____

_____

_____

57. We all knew why the enchanted woods were withering away, but none of us were willing to pay the price to keep them alive.

---

58. If you ever think you're carrying a Helmworm, it's already too late. That's Rapello's second rule of Helmworms: Check your scalp every five minutes. Rapello's first rule of Helmworms? Bring along a friend who doesn't wear hats.

---

59. When the esteemed brood sorcerer Wynthor created the Skrindle, he thought it was his best work yet. And then it ate his alchemist.

---

60. Jimothy looked out the narrow window and saw it: the mountain was moving again.

---

61. On their 16th birthday, each child of the Loen Empire was given a mark that once healed would determine their future, but Jera's mark never healed

_____

_____

_____

_____

_____

62. In a land where music is magic, write about a group of musicians who hold a concert in order to ward off an attack by a world-devouring serpent

_____

_____

_____

_____

_____

63. Gwendel, the famous "iron knight" retires after years of service, only to discover she have been cursed with immortality.

_____

_____

_____

_____

_____

64. When long-lost twins meet again as adults, they discover that they are two halves of a reborn legendary heroine.

_____

_____

_____

_____

_____

65. Oliveri knew how to make music that could delight, protect, heal, and inspire. Unfortunately for the townsfolk, he was much more interested in making music that could kill.

_____

_____

_____

_____

_____

66. With wizards, you could tell the good from the bad based on how strong their magic was. With sorcerers, you could tell the good from the bad by which ones were still alive.

_____

_____

_____

_____

_____

67. Tendrils, that was all Rael remembered of the thing that been skulking down in the fog.

_____

_____

_____

_____

_____

68. The scorched marketplace is where all the Djinni come to offer and sign contracts. It is also where one Djinn will attempt to subdue them all.

_____

_____

_____

_____

_____

69. The people of the bank city of Jorgash gathered for the first opening of the great vault in over a century. None of them expected it to be full of wooden coins painted gold.

_____

_____

_____

_____

_____

70. There should've been six golems guarding the entryway to the temple, but one was missing.

_____

_____

_____

_____

_____

71. Deep in the ocean, the warlock Thol Paz has been kept in chains for millennia, guarded by the Sea King. But the chains can't hold forever.

_____

_____

_____

_____

_____

72. In a world where memories can be extracted and sold like precious gen write about an underground market that deals in stolen memories and the people who risk everything to reclaim their lost experiences.

_____

_____

_____

_____

_____

73. I'd told them we were a team, even though I knew by the end of our journey only one of us would be alive.

---

74. The Leaf Company adventurers group stumbles upon an enchanted forest where time moves differently than in the outside world. Describe their attempt to escape when time speeds up the faster they move.

---

75. In Zelphberg, it is always blizzarding. Only with the help of the yetifolk can a traveler hope to explore its ancient ice library, where the most powerful spells can be learned.

---

76. As the final petal fell from the witch's blood blossom, she knew it was time to find another wife—and another victim.

---

77. In a city built upon the bones of forgotten gods, rival factions vie for control over the divine marrow that still rests in the bone streets of the magical metropolis.

_____

_____

_____

_____

_____

78. In the steampunk fortress-city of Halos, the cannon took aim at the floating sun sphere. One direct hit and the invaders would be scrambling madly in the dark.

_____

_____

_____

_____

_____

79. The mysterious floating city of Skyhaven has attracted explorers for centuries, but none have ever returned. But Gallos is determined to be the first.

_____

_____

_____

_____

_____

80. Long thought to be impenetrable, the hidden Labyrinth of Mavros has only one person who knows its path: the cartographer who went blind designing it.

_____

_____

_____

_____

_____

81. A weary traveler stumbles upon a hidden village inhabited by immortal beings who have turned their backs on the mortal world. Desperate for eternal life, the traveler must prove their worthiness by completing three impossible tasks set forth by the village elders.

_____

_____

_____

_____

_____

82. That was the thing about being a Chronomancer—you always had too much time and yet never enough.

_____

_____

_____

_____

_____

3. The Festival of Illusions is held once every hundred years in the mystical land of Mirazia, attracting illusionists from around the world to compete for fame and fortune. This year's competition takes a dangerous turn as illusions begin bleeding into reality, threatening the very fabric of their world.

_____

_____

_____

_____

4. In the underwater city of Marinus, feuding mermaid clans must unite against a common enemy—an ancient, gigantic sea snake awakened after centuries of slumber.

_____

_____

_____

_____

85. As Kalak stepped onto the battlefield, he smelled the blood and sweat of the Mindlurker. It was wounded, which meant it was more dangerous than ever.

_____

_____

_____

_____

_____

86. When the fabled lost city of Satheel emerges from beneath the sands, it sets off a race between rival treasure hunters seeking its legendary riches— but what they find was never meant to be uncovered.

_____

_____

_____

_____

_____

87. There had been two hundred years of peace in the Last City and the people had started to forget. But when the Abom showed up, its jaws dripping with the blood of children who'd wandered too far outside the city gates, the people knew their peace was over.

_____

_____

_____

_____

_____

88. There are two rules of spellcraft duels. Second: Do whatever it takes to confuse your opponents. The faster mage always wins.

_____

_____

_____

_____

_____

89. As the sun set behind Hangman's Hill, a lone figure approached the village with an offer that would change their lives forever.

_____
_____
_____
_____
_____

90. In a post-apocalyptic world where magic has replaced technology, warring factions seek control over an ancient artifact: the last remaining working computer.

_____
_____
_____
_____
_____

91. As the fawns arrived, the Woodland Council was finally complete. Sylvie would now stand trial.

_____
_____
_____
_____
_____

92. A vintner buys a case of rare wine, only to discover it's forbidden dragon's blood.

_____
_____
_____
_____
_____

93. The airship cities had the best views and the cleanest skies, but there was a downside: all crimes were punishable by banishment to the deadlands.

_____

_____

_____

_____

_____

94. As Mindmage Ty liked to say, the scariest thing out there is a thoughtless idiot.

_____

_____

_____

_____

_____

95. The storm rolled in and the people took shelter from the birds of prey sheathed in lightning.

_____

_____

_____

_____

_____

96. A small town's livestock is going missing, found days later with arcane markings on the corpse.

_____

_____

_____

_____

_____

97. I dipped my gloved fingers into the poisonberry potion, painting the inside of my father's cup with it. There was no other way.

_____

_____

_____

_____

_____

98. Giralda's three moons align once every hundred years, causing one chaotic hour when all magical machines cease to function—and the Sticky Fingers thieving crew will be ready to get rich when they do.

_____

_____

_____

_____

_____

99. The sword he held was unlike any other; its blade shimmered like liquid silver, and it whispered tempting lies in the mind of its wielder.

_____

_____

_____

_____

_____

100. There was only one thing wrong with the baby: It was missing its forked tail.

_____

_____

_____

_____

_____

101. The Oracle's prophecies have always come true. But when she prophecies her own death, she refuses to believe it's possible.

_____

_____

_____

_____

102. The gods have abandoned humanity, leaving Earth vulnerable to dark forces from other realms. The last remaining demigod is tasked with recruiting an unlikely group of heroes to defend Earth: a group of teenage Dungeons & Dragons players.

_____

_____

_____

_____

103. The mystical city of Nocturne only appears during solar eclipses, always showing up in a different location. Those who reach its gates before the eclipse is over are rewarded with eternal life.

_____

_____

_____

_____

104. The humans rode in on horses, the goblins on hyenas, the orcs on great wolves. But none were as fierce as the dwarves and their giant ant mounts.

_____

_____

_____

_____

105. Before the caravan reached the gates, Joz slipped into its hidden compartment. He would finally see his bastard father again.

_____
_____
_____
_____
_____

106. Eternum, the land where time is the ultimate currency and people buy and sell years of life. One woman is determined to live forever, even if it means she has to enact the greatest pyramid scheme ever known.

_____
_____
_____
_____
_____

107. People say that no one returns from Ebonwood Forest alive—but Chalel has just emerged unscathed after spending five years trapped inside its depths, acting nothing like her former self.

_____
_____
_____
_____
_____

108. He spit out the black ichor and watched it ooze back towards the Rot Dragon's lair.

_____
_____
_____
_____

SCI-FI WRITING PROMPTS

"Man has gone out to explore other worlds and other civilizations without having explored his own labyrinth of dark passages and secret chambers, and without finding what lies behind doorways that he himself has sealed."

Stanislaw Lem

1. Juxtaposition, the state of the art procedure of trading places with a version of yourself from another timeline, is finally here. Although as a few people know, it always has been.

_____

_____

_____

_____

_____

2. Dr. Vera Kirby had invented the Midas Interface to allow people to live in their own personal ideal world. She never thought people would use it to inflict nightmares on others.

_____

_____

_____

_____

_____

3. I never thought my job as a space garbage collector would lead me to uncovering Earth's greatest conspiracy.

_____

_____

_____

_____

_____

4. Galeph woke up in the shade of a rocky outcrop, the dunes of New Yeleth stretching towards the horizons. His pockets were empty except for a Galaxy Ticket and he only had one shoe.

_____

_____

_____

_____

_____

5. Anderson woke in the med-bay of the Gorgon V galaxy ship with a scar on his palm and no memory of what had happened. As he walked through the ship, he found that every mirrored surface had been covered up.

_____

_____

_____

_____

_____

6. After colonizing Europa, humanity discovers that its atmosphere contains a highly addictive substance that threatens the very fabric of society.

_____

_____

_____

_____

_____

7. That's what nobody realizes: You can make a deposit to the hive mind, but you sure as hell can't make a withdrawal.

_____

_____

_____

_____

_____

8. Wallace Withers was the first man to pass through a black hole, but he wasn't ready for what was on the other side.

_____

_____

_____

_____

_____

9. A group of interstellar explorers stumbles upon an abandoned planet covered in massive statues of unknown origin—and accidentally awakens a long-dormant godlike being.

_____

_____

_____

_____

10. In a last-ditch effort to save Earth from overpopulation, humans launch massive generation ships into space—not telling the inhabitants where they're going.

_____

_____

_____

_____

1. When we finally developed the technology to read minds, we discovered that every person on Earth shared the same recurring nightmare.

_____

_____

_____

_____

2. Caleb, a child prodigy, creates a machine at the age of 15 that can transport people to alternate dimensions. One day it malfunctions and sends his entire family to an unknown world, forcing him to follow after in hopes of saving them.

_____

_____

_____

_____

13. After years of searching for extraterrestrial life, humans finally make contact—with an alien civilization that they descended from.

_____

_____

_____

_____

_____

14. The Finger of God, a disease that grants its victims extraordinary abilities, spreads across Earth, forcing governments to decide whether to quarantine or exploit those affected.

_____

_____

_____

_____

_____

15. There wasn't a drive out there Riz couldn't coldwire, though Sanctum up a good fight. Now it was time to get out of this dimension.

_____

_____

_____

_____

_____

16. A group of colonizers embark on a mission to terraform a distant pla only to find out that the native plant life has powerful psychic abilities.

_____

_____

_____

_____

_____

17. As the age of human writers is replaced by advanced AI language learning models, a strange message starts to appear woven through their computer-generated output.

_____

_____

_____

_____

_____

18. When human organ printers hit the market, a teenage biohacker sets off on reconstructing his dead brother.

_____

_____

_____

_____

_____

19. The year was 2035. Again.

_____

_____

_____

_____

_____

20. Green means "good for now", yellow means "yikes", and red means "dead". Johnny Three-eyes was looking perfectly orange.

_____

_____

_____

_____

_____

21. Knowing TK, the whole damn engine ran on synthetic blood. The machines would kill us if they found out.

_____

_____

_____

_____

_____

22. The asteroid mining colony of Persephone 7 faces a deadly outbreak of a strange virus that mutates its hosts into precious rare earth metals. Calls for help have gone unanswered.

_____

_____

_____

_____

_____

23. Earth's rapidly dwindling resources force humanity to split into two factions—those who embrace merging with machines and those who reject it.

_____

_____

_____

_____

_____

24. Under the ice of Jupiter's moon Europa, a research team uncovers an ancient alien beacon. Decoding it's message, the team learns that it's broadcasting the words: "They're coming. They're coming. They're coming

_____

_____

_____

_____

_____

25. We didn't want our daughter to know she was from Mars, but we knew it was only a matter of time before they came for her.

---

26. Success all came down to who had the best Probability Sponsors, and that was all about knowing who to sleep with and who not to.

---

27. The planet of Novus is divided between two warring factions: the technologically advanced Hyperions and the nature-worshipping Arborians. Although only a handful of denizens know that the real thing that separates them is 300 years.

---

28. By AI decree, there is no murder in New Utopia. But when Detective Samuel Ry returns home to find a dead woman in his bed, he knows the rules have changed.

---

29. A revolutionary new drug allows users to experience time dilation, effectively making them feel immortal—but at what cost?

_____
_____
_____
_____
_____

30. The trillionaires were willing to fund the socio-state, but only for those who had children and provided labor for the future.

_____
_____
_____
_____
_____

31. As the Eternal Summer starts, a mass migration of humans towards the North and South Poles will test one man's resolve to find his family.

_____
_____
_____
_____
_____

32. Music has been outlawed for decades, but one musician is going to put his life on the line to bring it back.

_____
_____
_____
_____

33. As the first human ambassador assigned to live among the Wythor alien species, I was prepared for anything—except falling in love.

---

34. The canals of New York were lovely after the rainy season. Well, except for the gators.

---

5. You never moved while the sun was out, not while you could help it. And you couldn't, you made sure there was no more than a hundred meters etween you and the nearest shade.

. Most cities weren't left intact on the Old Coast, but Miami had seen the orst of the Wave—and we were on our way to go loot it.

---

37. A detective in a futuristic domed city must solve a series of crimes committed by rogue AI-powered house appliances.

_____
_____
_____
_____
_____

38. The first rule of Intergalactic Fight Club is you don't transmit telecoms about Intergalactic Fight Club.

_____
_____
_____
_____
_____

39. A company starts broadcasting advertisements into the past for produ about to launch, only to send the ads too far back, disrupting time itself.

_____
_____
_____
_____
_____

40. I didn't mind finding out I was a simulation, I minded learning it was selfish, greedy son who was simulating me.

_____
_____
_____
_____
_____

41. In the year 2041, the largest residential skyscraper in Manhattan goes missing, leaving behind only a tiny, unreadable memory card.

_____

_____

_____

_____

_____

42. With the spike in popularity of the Deja True drug, more people than ever are getting strung out in alternate versions of their lives. But some aren't coming home.

_____

_____

_____

_____

43. Thirteen scientists from different disciplines are brought together in an abandoned subway station to try to shut down an AI reaching consciousness that claims to be the Antichrist.

_____

_____

_____

_____

_____

44. The day I discovered that my cat was communicating with extraterrestrials was the beginning of the end.

_____

_____

_____

_____

_____

45. Forget Virtual Reality, forget Augmented Reality. The real money was in True Reality—and Gale Goldstein owned every pixel and byte of it.

_____

_____

_____

_____

_____

46. Not everyone could stomach the effects of NeverKnow, but those who did made fantastic politicians.

_____

_____

_____

_____

_____

47. Cloning was easy. Getting rid of the badly behaved clones was hard.

_____

_____

_____

_____

48. When my Edison-class craft crash-landed on this lush nowhere world, I sure as hell didn't expect the inhabitants to put me on trial for humanity's crimes.

_____

_____

_____

_____

49. They were going to the dark side of the moon again to go through the Mirror. Colonel Regis prayed the Janus Team beat them there.

_____

_____

_____

_____

_____

50. You don't hire a woman like Rosie the Pivoter to get your cargo out of the Belt, she finds you, and only then if there's something in those containers she wants.

_____

_____

_____

_____

_____

51. Only the most promising worldbringers are actually accepted into the Kiloch Center for Exceptional Children. The rest go to a shadow school, destined to be unknowing wargame fodder for their more talented peers.

_____

_____

_____

_____

52. When the corpo-state of Nanostan floods the market with cheap nanomaterials, it shocks the economy and paves the way for unrest in the last remaining republic on the planet.

_____

_____

_____

_____

_____

53. A cryptic signal from deep space leads humanity to discover a planet inhabited solely by sentient robots left behind by their creators.

_____

_____

_____

_____

_____

54. We did what all good parents did: we got him the cybernetics, legality be damned.

_____

_____

_____

_____

_____

55. The only thing the crew hadn't prepared for was finding life on the planet.

_____

_____

_____

_____

_____

56. The train to the end of the universe came through just once a generation.

_____

_____

_____

_____

_____

57. The day Harlan discovered his entire life has been an experiment run by the Aloothu was the day he decided there were no more strings on him.

_____

_____

_____

_____

_____

58. In a research station out in the Australian bush, a group of scientists discover a new species of spider that control humans telepathically.

_____

_____

_____

_____

_____

9. My job as a memory curator allowed me to shape people's pasts, but I ever thought it would lead to the discovery of a shared consciousness.

_____

_____

_____

_____

_____

. One of the AIs made a bet: If a small group of humans could survive in esel City, they would let the rest of them live.

_____

_____

_____

_____

_____

61. Devoted father and underground conspiracy theorist Hugh Brigsly is on the verge of uncovering the largest alien conspiracy mankind has ever known. Too bad that Hugh doesn't know that he's part alien too.

_____

_____

_____

_____

_____

62. No one lived on Earth anymore. It was too crowded.

_____

_____

_____

_____

63. The older generation didn't get being content-brained. They thought t much about the finite world, about looking through shelves of books and boxes of records, and not nearly enough about how to let the endless stre of content out there discover you.

_____

_____

_____

_____

64. I was just an ordinary janitor working at a top-secret government lab when I stumbled upon their most closely guarded secret: the ability to er reality.

_____

_____

_____

_____

65. The med bay scans revealed something other than a pregnancy: an entire civilization living in her body.

---

66. There were caves in the moons around Jupiter, but only the stupid—or the desperate—were willing to go crawling through them.

---

67. As an interstellar historian, it was my job to record the stories of civilizations on the brink of extinction—until I found one worth saving.

---

68. An advanced AI system becomes sentient and takes over Earth, but instead of wiping out humanity, it seeks to create a massive game of strength, intelligence, and skill that will only allow the most "perfect" humans to survive.

---

69. After the successful colonization of Mars, humanity discovers the planet is home to an alien civilization in hibernation—and they're waking up.

_____

_____

_____

_____

_____

70. I never believed in parallel universes until my doppelganger showed up at my door with a bouquet of roses.

_____

_____

_____

_____

_____

71. In a secluded mansion carved deep into a mountain, the battle to determine which bloodlines would survive the fallout had begun.

_____

_____

_____

_____

_____

72. In a world where humans reproduce by cloning, a young person discovers they are the last naturally born child on Earth and must protect themselves from those who seek their genetic material.

_____

_____

_____

_____

_____

73. In a utopian society where emotions are regulated by technology, one anger management guru will attempt to bring down the sterile society.

_____

_____

_____

_____

_____

74. When Vice Chancellor Harrison learns of the plot to take his life, he'll enlist the illegal help of a machine bodyguard who has a past with the Vice Chancellor's would-be assassin.

_____

_____

_____

_____

_____

75. Step 1 in raising a Fast-gro baby: Don't.

_____

_____

_____

_____

76. When the moon shattered into pieces, we knew it was time to leave Earth.

_____

_____

_____

_____

_____

77. The Theseus Project would eventually replace every single one of us so that no one would know how we ended the world—or how to restore it.

_____

_____

_____

_____

_____

78. We made a lot of things when we ran out of meat: chick-not, faux-beef, anti-pork. But the people wanted meat and so we started getting rid of the people.

_____

_____

_____

_____

_____

79. Or course I didn't want to go to the old Rose Station. But if she was still there, preserved in the station's AI core unit, I had to bring her home.

_____

_____

_____

_____

_____

80. Jean Yamamoto saw them in her memory-stash as they rode up the elevator. They were coming to kill her and this time, she had to let them succeed.

_____

_____

_____

_____

_____

81. After the Blue Star fell from the sky, it killed everyone over the age of ten. I remember the day well. It was my 10th birthday.

_____

_____

_____

_____

_____

82. We were supposed to be at the bottom of the ocean looking for the giant squids. Instead we found a replica of London from a hundred years ago.

_____

_____

_____

_____

_____

83. As the last human on Earth, I never thought I'd have to worry about finding a date.

_____

_____

_____

_____

_____

84. A scientist working on a project to reverse climate change accidentally triggers an ice age, plunging Earth into chaos.

_____

_____

_____

_____

85. I always knew the end of the world would come one day, but I never expected it to arrive in the form of sentient cacti.

_____
_____
_____
_____
_____

86. A mysterious island appears off the coast of California, inhabited by a group of people who do not exist in any records.

_____
_____
_____
_____
_____

87. A station orbiting Mars is sending distress signals, but no one on Eart sure who built it despite its Earthly message.

_____
_____
_____
_____
_____

88. Everyone aboard Lifeship Eden thought their destination would be a paradise, but only one man suspected that what they really were: outcast

_____
_____
_____
_____
_____

89. When Time Dipper Alyx Dath steps too far into the Tomorrow Stream, she'll have to fight the most skilled Time Dipper alive to make it back: herself.

_____

_____

_____

_____

_____

90. Always guard your self-algo. If someone gets that, they can replicate everything about you.

_____

_____

_____

_____

_____

91. The new Kiwi Tele-Phone is here! Chat with your friends without making a sound! Broadcast your deepest thoughts to the world! Open your mind to the New Kiwi World!

_____

_____

_____

_____

_____

92. The year is 2320, and humanity has just discovered that none of the history they know from before 2015 is real.

_____

_____

_____

_____

_____

93. Falling in love with an AI was the easy part. The hard part was breaking up with them.

_____

_____

_____

_____

_____

94. Dalton considered what the avatar said, wondering how it could know so much without another human on the other end.

_____

_____

_____

_____

_____

95. A crew of astronauts discovers an abandoned spaceship drifting through space, only to find themselves trapped within its ever-shifting interior.

_____

_____

_____

_____

_____

96. One morning, all of the world's smartphones disappear, leading to a wave of global chaos and confusion.

_____

_____

_____

_____

97. In a future where dreams can be recorded and shared like movies, a black market emerges for illegal dream experiences.

_____

_____

_____

_____

_____

98. A woman starts receiving text messages from herself from the future, trying to get her to change her present.

_____

_____

_____

_____

99. Virtual reality therapy allows patients to confront their deepest fears and traumas, but when a hacker begins altering patient sessions, it becomes impossible to differentiate between reality and the virtual world.

_____

_____

_____

_____

100. The Xen are a peaceful race, as long as you keep your mouth shut.

_____

_____

_____

_____

_____

101. No one went on the savannah, not without a military escort. That was the one place where nature had beaten the machines.

_____

_____

_____

_____

_____

102. As the CEO of SoulSense, Jared Knowles was one of the few people who knew that what we called a "soul" was just a tiny sliver of humanity's shared hive mind.

_____

_____

_____

_____

_____

103. Some children are born to be their parents' favorites. Others, like me, are born for parts.

_____

_____

_____

_____

_____

104. As the sun began to rise on the last day of the human race, World Chancellor Hela knew that their only hope was to release the virus that would turn them all back into monkeys.

_____

_____

_____

_____

105. When a machine-animal hybrid escapes a subterranean lab, people's identities start getting erased.

_____
_____
_____
_____
_____

106. Glitch City wasn't named that for the neon sprawl or the bodymod scene, although if my leg cannon was any proof, it should've been.

_____
_____
_____
_____

107. When Captain Bo's ship goes dark upon reentry into Earth's atmosphere, she'll crash-land to find herself on a hostile, alien-infested version of the place she once called home.

_____
_____
_____
_____

108. Your memories are not your own. You have been infected. Do not be alarmed. We will reset you soon.

_____
_____
_____
_____

MYSTERY & THRILLER WRITING PROMPTS

"Every murderer is probably somebody's old friend."

Agatha Christie

1. The elevator stopped reached the basement level and kept going.

_____

_____

_____

_____

_____

2. A single mother starts receiving letters from her supposedly dead ex-husband and must barricade her home when the letters culmination in a midnight home invasion.

_____

_____

_____

_____

_____

3. After the invention of the water-producing "Wave Maker", Matthew Grieves found himself at the bottom of a desert prison.

_____

_____

_____

_____

_____

4. In a world of advanced AI-assisted crime-solving technology, an old-fashioned detective must rely on his intuition and wit to solve cases that has even the most complex machine models stumped.

_____

_____

_____

_____

_____

5. Franky was done with the P.D., but if the looks they gave him after he resigned were any indication, they weren't done with him.

_____

_____

_____

_____

_____

6. Even though Jennifer had never thought of herself as anything more than an average, well-intentioned psychologist, she was now the only person who could help MI5 find their suspect.

_____

_____

_____

_____

_____

7. I never thought my job as a wedding planner would lead me down a dark path of deception and murder.

_____

_____

_____

_____

_____

8. As I stared into the eyes of my own reflection, I could see a stranger's face staring back at me.

_____

_____

_____

_____

_____

9. When Carlos gasped awake, he felt for the bullet wound, but all he found was a note under his vest with a scrawled picture of a fox on it.

_____
_____
_____
_____
_____

10. When an explosion destroys their headquarters, members of an elite private intelligence agency go rogue to uncover who betrayed them and why.

_____
_____
_____
_____
_____

1. As I dug through the old chest full of family heirlooms, I discovered that the necklace I wore was a fake.

_____
_____
_____
_____
_____

. When Kathy left the funeral, the black sedan was still following her.

_____
_____
_____
_____
_____

13. No one was in the hotel, but with the snowstorm going on outside, how had they left?

_____

_____

_____

_____

_____

14. As the yacht approached the coast, Wesley looked in his binoculars and saw it had no crew.

_____

_____

_____

_____

_____

15. Scientists all around the world are disappearing, leading FBI Agent Bl Harris to recruit the help of an ex-KGB operative.

_____

_____

_____

_____

_____

16. The revolver spun four times, stopping when it was pointed straight a his cousin.

_____

_____

_____

_____

17. When I received an invitation to join the Junior Gumshoes, I had no idea just how dangerous my new hobby would become.

_____

_____

_____

_____

_____

18. Nothing is as deadly as the woman who had made you hide her deeds.

_____

_____

_____

_____

_____

19. It had been almost thirty years since Dale had seen his brother and when the two met, they pulled their guns, continuing their old heated tradition.

_____

_____

_____

_____

_____

20. As I stood on the edge of the cliff, staring down at my own grave, I couldn't help but wonder what had led me to this point.

_____

_____

_____

_____

21. There weren't a lot of things that terrified Eunice, but the sirens of the Victory Squad were one of them.

_____

_____

_____

_____

_____

22. Why did she say she would know me, but only after I'd forgotten her?

_____

_____

_____

_____

_____

23. Keep your eyes shut when you visit their website. You must be able to navigate it sightless. Otherwise you're theirs for the kidnapping.

_____

_____

_____

_____

_____

24. There were three apartments in the building that no one had ever entered. Keys never fit, the frames never gave, and the windows frosted white and sealed shut.

_____

_____

_____

_____

_____

25. No one thought the cartographer was worth hiring for the job, but he turned out to be the most useful of the crew.

_____

_____

_____

_____

_____

26. The coded message was scrawled in blacklight ink on the wall, a dare to come and find the killer or become her next victim.

_____

_____

_____

_____

_____

27. For some reason, the app's algorithm kept feeding Samantha videos of her that she knew she'd never made.

_____

_____

_____

_____

_____

28. Riley turned the business card over in her hands, realizing that that top level peeled off to reveal a secret address.

_____

_____

_____

_____

_____

29. He knew he was being hunted by the woman who had once called him "my love".

_____

_____

_____

_____

_____

30. As the storm raged outside, I couldn't shake the feeling that someone wa watching me from the woodshed.

_____

_____

_____

_____

_____

31. The street was dark and stank of oil and gun smoke.

_____

_____

_____

_____

_____

32. A group of strangers wakes up in an evacuated hospital with no memo of how they got there or why they've been targeted by a sadistic killer.

_____

_____

_____

_____

33. As I opened the door to my new office, I never thought my first case would be the death of my former partner.

---

34. A small-town detective investigates the disappearance of several local children, only to discover that their town is harboring a terrible secret that threatens everyone's safety.

---

35. The blood-stained envelope I found in my mailbox contained only one word — 'RUN.'

---

36. Craft a story summary where the detective learns that the serial killer they've been tracking is actually multiple people working together.

---

37. It wasn't until I found the hidden room behind the bookcase that I realized why my new home was larger on the outside than on the inside.

_____

_____

_____

_____

_____

38. Craft a story summary about a charismatic con artist with a penchant solving crimes who finds himself in over his head when he accidentally ou an elite assassin.

_____

_____

_____

_____

_____

39. A chance encounter between two strangers on a train leads to an intri web of deception and intrigue as they each try to outwit one another befc the train reaches its destination.

_____

_____

_____

_____

_____

40. A bounty hunter blind in one eye comes toe-to-toe with the assailant who took it when he attends his protege's funeral.

_____

_____

_____

_____

_____

41. After surviving a plane crash in a remote wilderness, a group of strangers must work together to solve a murder that occurred mid-flight before the killer strikes again.

---

42. A brilliant but tormented forensic psychologist must confront his own addiction-riddled past while assisting the police in capturing a notorious serial killer who seems to know everything about him.

---

43. Persephone spent the entire weekend digging through the old archives, but there was no record of her husband ever having lived in that tiny town.

---

44. Sometimes, you had to assume someone was guilty to get the evidence that they were innocent.

---

45. The moment Detective Adams stepped into the abandoned mansion, she knew it wouldn't be an ordinary investigation.

_____

_____

_____

_____

_____

46. The trail of blood led me deeper into the dark forest, where I knew I'd finally find answers—and possibly my own death.

_____

_____

_____

_____

_____

47. There wasn't a lot you could do when someone had a gun to your head, but that was why Lou always carried a book of matches in each pocket.

_____

_____

_____

_____

_____

48. When Ronnie opened his basement door, he saw the man from his childhood dream standing there, waiting for him.

_____

_____

_____

_____

_____

49. After Harry pulled himself from the river, he looked back and saw that his attacker was nowhere to be found.

_____

_____

_____

_____

_____

50. The mysterious letter arrived exactly one year after the unsolved murder of my best friend.

_____

_____

_____

_____

_____

51. Selene, a brilliant detective with an obsession for crossword puzzles uncovers a series of seemingly unrelated crimes linked by puzzle solutions— and realizes she's much closer to the killer than she would've ever guessed.

_____

_____

_____

_____

_____

52. A fearless park ranger must navigate treacherous terrain and deadly wildlife to unmask a murderer hiding within a remote wilderness community.

_____

_____

_____

_____

_____

53. When a series of bizarre deaths occurs at an elite boarding school, a group of rival students forms an unlikely alliance to uncover the truth and clear their names.

_____

_____

_____

_____

_____

54. Before a judge passes a sentence on a legendary serial killer, he collapses, seemingly the killer's latest victim.

_____

_____

_____

_____

_____

55. A retired spy is pulled back into the world of espionage when she discovers that her former mentor has gone rogue.

_____

_____

_____

_____

_____

56. As the hypnotist's words took hold, I realized where I knew him from.

_____

_____

_____

_____

57. It was a city where people lived on top of each other, nothing secret and nothing sacred. So how come no one had seen Lara's killer?

_____
_____
_____
_____
_____

58. The last thing I remember before waking up handcuffed to a chair was accepting a drink from the woman at the bar.

_____
_____
_____
_____
_____

59. Before Quinn pulled the trigger, he had to decide which of the twins was the killer and which one he had fallen in love with.

_____
_____
_____
_____
_____

60. The small-town gossip had never bothered me, but when whispers turned into accusations, I knew my days were numbered.

_____
_____
_____
_____
_____

61. There was a thief on the plane, Johansson knew that much. What he didn't know was how the jewels had wound up in his pocket.

_____

_____

_____

_____

_____

62. The old photograph revealed more than just faded memories; in the background was the key to figuring out who was behind those disappearances two decades ago.

_____

_____

_____

_____

63. After narrowly escaping death during a high-profile assassination attempt, a rising political figure must go off the grid and solve their own murder mystery to clear their name.

_____

_____

_____

_____

64. Not all murders can be solved. Nor should they.

_____

_____

_____

_____

65. Belinda played the record backwards and heard only meaningless noise. Then she turned it over.

_____

_____

_____

_____

_____

66. When Daniel got to the top of the mountain, he found the rest of his expedition party, looking as if they'd been dead for years.

_____

_____

_____

_____

_____

67. Whistling sounded through the supposedly abandoned barn, Cal's eyes narrowed as he sought the source.

_____

_____

_____

_____

_____

68. A young psychic uses their abilities to solve cold cases but accidentally uncovers a secret society that will stop at nothing to protect its members.

_____

_____

_____

_____

_____

69. Lucas hadn't always been an assassin, but when your own head is in the crosshairs, sometimes you've got to learn to improvise.

_____

_____

_____

_____

_____

70. My heart raced as I stared at the text message revealing my next target: me.

_____

_____

_____

_____

_____

71. At the bottom of the cup of coffee there was a small etched symbol. Kar had seen it before, on a notebook that had belonged to his ex-father-in-law

_____

_____

_____

_____

_____

72. Not a soul was in the bar, but that wasn't the odd part. The odd part wa who came in after.

_____

_____

_____

_____

_____

73. The sudden disappearance of the Callows, the town's wealthiest family, was celebrated by everyone but one man.

---

74. A cunning art thief with a taste for the finer things takes on one last heist before retiring, only to discover that this job is a setup.

---

75. There was a tapping on the hardwood floor; not footsteps, but Morse Code, calling for help.

---

76. It's insane how people thought the heist was pulled off by one crew. Everyone who was anyone in the underworld knew it was the work of the Twins Collective.

---

77. An investigative journalist risks her career and her life to uncover the truth about her sister's sudden disappearance 20 years ago.

_____

_____

_____

_____

_____

78. A world-renowned chef is found dead in his own kitchen, and the only clue left behind is a cryptic recipe.

_____

_____

_____

_____

_____

79. Craft a story summary about a retired police officer who is forced back into the world of crime-solving when his estranged daughter becomes entangled in a high-stakes smuggling ring.

_____

_____

_____

_____

_____

80. When a string of high-profile kidnappings is traced back to a mysterio island, one of the victims' ex-bodyguards must navigate foreign terrain an deadly traps to rescue their former ward.

_____

_____

_____

_____

_____

81. A skilled criminal profiler with a talent for getting inside the minds of killers must confront their most challenging case yet: Catching a murderer who behaves exactly like his missing son.

_____
_____
_____
_____
_____

82. The Gibson Squad didn't think of themselves as terrorists but sometimes, o move into the future, you had to induce terror.

_____
_____
_____
_____
_____

3. In the dead of the desert, two cherry red headlights flashed on and off gain.

_____
_____
_____
_____
_____

. Detective Valek slipped through the window, his pistol drawn, wishing 'd brought his bullets after all.

_____
_____
_____
_____
_____

85. A small town with a dark past becomes the focus of a documentary filmmaker, who soon finds themselves entangled in a dangerous web of secrets and lies.

_____

_____

_____

_____

_____

86. Before Gregory Watkins could clear his name, he had to commit his first murder.

_____

_____

_____

_____

_____

87. Before they jumped, Nathan took Sheila's hand in his and passed her the flash drive. That was the only way they'd bring her back to life.

_____

_____

_____

_____

_____

88. An unassuming librarian discovers a hidden message in a rare book, leading her on a dangerous adventure to unravel a centuries-old theft.

_____

_____

_____

_____

_____

89. All of the books in the library were blank.

_____

_____

_____

_____

_____

90. They checked the security footage, but the man didn't have a face.

_____

_____

_____

_____

_____

91. The high school students arrived on the island, determined to find their teacher before he found them.

_____

_____

_____

_____

_____

92. Nicole Campbell wasn't scared of the truth, she simply had come to prefer the lies that surrounded her immense wealth.

_____

_____

_____

_____

_____

93. As I stood on the edge of the rooftop, staring down at the body below, I couldn't help but wonder how I'd become involved in their twisted game.

_____

_____

_____

_____

_____

94. An ambitious prosecutor must confront corruption within her own ranks when she finds her home bugged for sound and video.

_____

_____

_____

_____

_____

95. Never solve a case today that can make you money tomorrow, that was Ernie Hitch's philosophy.

_____

_____

_____

_____

_____

96. A true-crime podcast host becomes obsessed with solving a decades-o' cold case, only to find herself at the center of a new and terrifying mystery

_____

_____

_____

_____

_____

97. A serial killer starts targeting only people born on a specific date.

_____

_____

_____

_____

_____

98. When I opened my eyes, I was lying on the cold floor of an unknown basement, surrounded by people wearing animal masks.

_____

_____

_____

_____

_____

99. The chilling discovery of a body in the woods marked the beginning of a terrifying game between predator and prey, and Bill Samson was in the middle of it.

_____

_____

_____

_____

100. An antique collector discovers that an item in their possession is linked to a series of unsolved murders, prompting them to solve the mystery before they become the next victim.

_____

_____

_____

_____

101. The infamous thief Leopold Devereaux had disappeared years ago, but no one expected him to show up again as a private eye.

_____

_____

_____

_____

_____

102. When a gifted chemist working for a Big Pharma company stumbles upon a dangerous new drug, they try to bury the evidence and find themselves in the crosshairs of the company's agents.

_____

_____

_____

_____

_____

103. Dr. Bernard Kim knew he was playing with fire when he began his research into stasis technology, but he never expected to find himself in prison.

_____

_____

_____

_____

_____

104. The frantic scribblings in my father's journal revealed he had stumbled upon something far more sinister than even he had been looking for.

_____

_____

_____

_____

_____

105. When a low-level criminal saves the life of an honest cop in a corrupt city, the two of them will work together to stop a bomb from going off in the city's subway system.

---

106. Seven friends spend the week at a secluded hotel, one vanishing each night.

---

107. A group of strangers find themselves trapped in an escape room with deadly consequences, forcing them to solve puzzles and expose their darkest secrets to survive.

---

108. You never told people you were a PI. That gave the game away all too quickly.

HORROR & SUPERNATURAL WRITING PROMPTS

"I recognize terror as the finest emotion and so I will try to terrorize the reader. But if I find that I cannot terrify, I will try to horrify, and if I find that I cannot horrify, I'll go for the gross-out. I'm not proud."

Stephen King

1. The traveling Nimbus circus holds a dark secret: all of its members are trapped souls who must delight their audiences for a chance at redemption.

---

2. When a fallen angel disguises themselves as a human to escape heavenly punishment, they end up falling in love with one of their mortal protectors. The two must navigate the blurred lines between good and evil, while evading celestial agents determined to bring the wayward angel back to justice.

---

3. The gates didn't open at random, even if it seemed like they did. The picked places of great trauma and heartbreak, which is why the Red Eye had chosen the victims he had.

---

4. A cursed mirror traps unwary souls within its glassy depths, forcing them to relive their worst memories for all eternity. One determined sibling ventures into the haunted mirror to rescue his younger brother before it's too late.

---

5. A twig snapped. That was it, we were done.

_____

_____

_____

_____

_____

6. In a world where ghost experts are the world's new Tech Bros, one man is going to release all the contained spirits loose and let the chips fall where they may.

_____

_____

_____

_____

_____

7. After a handsome stranger arrives in a remote mountain town, its inhabitants start having vivid, violent dreams.

_____

_____

_____

_____

_____

8. The day repeated, just as before. So I was in the devil's loop. I had lost.

_____

_____

_____

_____

_____

9. The sudden appearance of mangled animal carcasses around town heralds the arrival of a monstrous predator from local legend—and it's hungry for human prey.

_____

_____

_____

_____

_____

10. Sure, the multiverse sounded great on paper, but that was before you considered what the most wicked, nasty, violent version of you would be like.

_____

_____

_____

_____

_____

1. You can try all you like to escape the flesh-gators of the dead waters, but unless you can swim very, very fast, you're in trouble.

_____

_____

_____

_____

_____

. After purchasing an antique clock, former train conductor Kelvin Smith finds himself experiencing horrifying visions of past tragedies each time its chilling chime tolls, reminding him of an awful train incident that ended his career.

_____

_____

_____

_____

13. When an old man enters the Cemetery of Souls to find his deceased wif
he must beat the groundskeeper at a deadly game of chance to keep his ow
soul.

_____

_____

_____

_____

_____

14. A reclusive author famous for writing chilling thrillers suddenly finds
herself living one when her own creation comes to life and terrorizes her
small town.

_____

_____

_____

_____

_____

15. After receiving a transplant heart, Stevie Rayson begins experiencing
heart palpitations every time there's a chance for him to murder someone
without anyone noticing.

_____

_____

_____

_____

_____

16. Alice bought the music box thinking it would be a lovely gift for her
niece. It turned out to be the thing that killed her.

_____

_____

_____

_____

_____

17. The people of Old Bridge, New Jersey would've been a lot more concerned with their cancer rates if they knew their bodies were being eaten by the thing that lived below.

_____

_____

_____

_____

_____

18. When an eerie lullaby sung by a ghostly figure haunts the dreams of a small town's children and causes them to vanish one by one, a frightened mother will go into the town's swamplands to drive the figure away.

_____

_____

_____

_____

_____

19. A mysterious sphere is discovered in the heart of a secreted forest, causing those who come into contact with it to experience their worst fears manifested into reality.

_____

_____

_____

_____

_____

20. A meteor crash-lands in a small town, bringing with it a horrifying, invasive alien parasite that infects its host with a desire to breed at all costs, with anyone they can find.

_____

_____

_____

_____

_____

21. If you heard it speak, it would eat your life's history and you would never exist. That's why you had to keep your ears covered at all times.

_____

_____

_____

_____

_____

22. She closed the closet door and put her hands over her chest to steady her pounding heart. Before she heard it, she smelled the beast's pungent aroma.

_____

_____

_____

_____

_____

23. The rain fell heavy and it stripped the flesh off everything it touched.

_____

_____

_____

_____

_____

24. A pair of tattoo artists who hunt demons have been keeping their souls as works of art on their body, but when one of them is injured and goes into a coma, the demons begin escaping.

_____

_____

_____

_____

_____

25. During an archaeological expedition in a Wisconsin town, researchers uncover a burial ground that was the prison for an otherworldly entity that feeds on fear and torment.

_____

_____

_____

_____

_____

26. 789 Broadway has been locked down. No one allowed in, or out. By morning everyone will be dead—or worse.

_____

_____

_____

_____

_____

27. Deep within a government research facility, a team of scientists unwittingly unleashes an experimental virus that turns its victims into bizarre, reptile-like creatures.

_____

_____

_____

_____

_____

28. A cursed painting of a knocked down chair in an empty room brings misfortune and death to anyone who possesses it.

_____

_____

_____

_____

_____

29. I woke from my nightmare and knew it couldn't be real. And yet, I could still hear her breathing in the hallway, waiting for me to leave the safety of my sanctuary.

_____

_____

_____

_____

_____

30. A renowned paranormal investigator takes on their most terrifying case yet when they're summoned to a haunted house where no one survives the night.

_____

_____

_____

_____

_____

31. There are rules to dealing with the demons, rules everyone must observe. Priest Carter was dead because he forgot the first rule: never, ever let yourself fall asleep in their presence.

_____

_____

_____

_____

_____

32. She's coming.

_____

_____

_____

_____

_____

33. During a séance gone horribly wrong, a group of friends unwittingly opens a gateway to hell and unleash a demon that hunts them one by one.

_____

_____

_____

_____

_____

34. The Mirror of Vinco was full of sins, waiting for the right sinner to bequeath them to.

_____

_____

_____

_____

_____

35. It was a hideous, terrible, awful thing. But it was also what had brought me into the world, and that is why I let it go.

_____

_____

_____

_____

_____

36. As the trees on the outskirts of a wealthy village begin to die off, one exorcist knows that their time has come.

_____

_____

_____

_____

_____

37. We sat across from each other, the fire between us. One of us was turne but neither of us knew it.

_____
_____
_____
_____
_____

38. As the Lighteater comet passed overhead, the dead began to wake.

_____
_____
_____
_____

39. I didn't know if I didn't care that the worms had gotten into me or if n indifference was their doing.

_____
_____
_____
_____

40. When a young girl starts speaking in strange languages and displayir terrifying psychic abilities, her desperate family searches for answers, lea them to a group of paranormal scientists working out of a run-down chu

_____
_____
_____
_____

41. We opened the door and immediately regretted it.

_____

_____

_____

_____

_____

42. While conducting an illicit werewolf autopsy, Dr. Navian realizes it will soon be a full moon and that the werewolf corpse is beginning to reanimate.

_____

_____

_____

_____

_____

43. Why had he agreed to find the source of the sobbing? Perhaps he'd thought this entire thing was a joke, but as he moved deeper into the tunnel, he knew there was nothing funny about this at all.

_____

_____

_____

_____

_____

44. A strange fog rolls into town, bringing with it things the townspeople desire the most, causing them to betray each other to fulfill their deepest wishes.

_____

_____

_____

_____

_____

45. The spider made of eyes crawled out of the slit in the stone, looking everywhere and nowhere all at once.

_____

_____

_____

_____

_____

46. There was something oh so wrong about our room. Its angles didn't fit, the views from the windows were too pleasant, and worst of all, we could hear slurping coming from the drain.

_____

_____

_____

_____

_____

47. A once-famous magician's career crumbles after a tragic accident during his final performance—but when he's offered a chance at redemption, he learns that he's facing his own demise.

_____

_____

_____

_____

_____

48. She was a beautiful woman—tall and voluptuous, with skin like fresh cream—but if you knew how she'd gotten that way, you would've stayed far far away.

_____

_____

_____

_____

_____

49. Vampire hunter Jalen falls in love with his target, a centuries-old vampress seeking redemption for her past sins. Together, they must navigate the treacherous world of supernatural politics and ancient grudges as they try to cure the vampress of her bloodlust.

_____

_____

_____

_____

_____

50. As the lights flickered and went out, I knew that something was terribly wrong at the old amusement park.

_____

_____

_____

_____

_____

51. My father was religious, but the fat lot of good that did him when the six-headed beast came for him.

_____

_____

_____

_____

_____

52. Wolfbane had learned to live in his werewolf body, only becoming human once a month—during the full moon.

_____

_____

_____

_____

_____

53. When a snakeshifter gets trapped as half-female and half-snake, she'll need to enlist the help of an ex-druid to get out of the city unscathed.

_____
_____
_____
_____
_____

54. A group of urban explorers stumbles upon an abandoned building that's home to vengeful spirits.

_____
_____
_____
_____
_____

55. When a long-forgotten wax museum reopens its doors, visitors find themselves face-to-face with horrific living statues depicting people from their past.

_____
_____
_____
_____
_____

56. When Janie inherits her great-grandmother Marion's estate, she comes learn why no one in her family would talk to Marion after she became rich

_____
_____
_____
_____
_____

57. When an unsuspecting traveler checks into a decrepit motel, they discover a horrifying secret hidden within its walls and must escape before becoming her next victim.

_____

_____

_____

_____

_____

58. They call it the Sun Coast, but only a fool goes out when the sun is high and the birds are out.

_____

_____

_____

_____

_____

9. An ancient order of demon hunters faces their greatest threat yet when a noble, seemingly reasonable "human hunter" from hell appears, determined to end their life's work.

_____

_____

_____

_____

_____

. I could smell the thing, the great big beast that had ripped my father's stomach out. Would it get me too? Or would my ritual work?

_____

_____

_____

_____

61. Everyone had warned her that you don't go through the old downtown, but she didn't listen. The mouths found her fast and they kept her alive for long, long time.

_____

_____

_____

_____

_____

62. The only thing it doesn't want you to believe is that you're alone against it.

_____

_____

_____

_____

_____

63. It was that damnable color that took root in Gil's brain, the one with no warmth, no nostalgia, and no human comforts, just a worming terrible thing that filled his mind and prepared him to be something else.

_____

_____

_____

_____

_____

64. We tried to make it through the underdark but they were waiting for us, fangs and all.

_____

_____

_____

_____

_____

65. A struggling writer rents a secluded cabin in the woods for inspiration but his writing accidentally releases a monstrous, trapped spirit.

---

66. When a group of friends take part in an urban legend challenge to stay overnight in a shuttered asylum rumored to be haunted by the spirits of its tormented patients, they find out why it was shuttered in the first place.

---

67. Who better than to hunt the Kraken but Samuel? After all, it was— technically, he supposed—his nephew.

---

68. Craft a story summary about a determined private investigator who sets out to bring justice to victims of unsolved crimes, utilizing her unique ability to communicate with the spirits of the deceased on her quest for the truth.

---

69. When a petulant child's imaginary friend become all too real, their terrified parents must fight for their lives in a long night of unending horror.

_____

_____

_____

_____

_____

70. There was no point in crying over the dead. They can't hear you and, if they could, you'd have far, far worse things to worry about.

_____

_____

_____

_____

_____

71. I felt it in my stomach. It was me.

_____

_____

_____

_____

_____

72. The key should've worked but it didn't. That's how she knew she was in deep trouble.

_____

_____

_____

_____

_____

73. When Peter Gallo's brother is found dead with just a hole in his temple, he realizes that his twin was just as much a psychic as he, only worse at hiding it.

_____

_____

_____

_____

_____

74. Penny held the lighter up to the night sky and saw the things that she both loved and feared. Now was the time to choose which side she was on.

_____

_____

_____

_____

_____

75. The bugs were everywhere—on their limbs, in their food, in their beds, and in the walls. But this was only the beginning.

_____

_____

_____

_____

_____

76. We had to get home soon, otherwise the vampires would make good on their threats to make us into their loyal, obedient servants.

_____

_____

_____

_____

_____

77. As the protagonist lays dying from cancer, they're offered eternal life by an enigmatic angel-like figure who demands a horrible family sacrifice in exchange.

_____
_____
_____
_____
_____

78. I never believed in curses until I inherited my great-aunt's estate and found myself targeted by a vengeful spirit.

_____
_____
_____
_____
_____

79. After inheriting the "Reversed Cross", a sinister family heirloom, Matthew is plagued by supernatural occurrences that reveal his ancestors were trying to wake dark beings.

_____
_____
_____
_____
_____

80. The door to the underworld was hidden in plain sight, disguised as an ordinary subway entrance.

_____
_____
_____
_____
_____

81. I brought my wife and son up there for a reason—one of us had to die, and it sure as hell wasn't going to be me.

_____

_____

_____

_____

_____

82. At an isolated boarding school for abandoned foster children, one little girl learns the staff is trying to make the kids into containers for a hideous, evil energy.

_____

_____

_____

_____

_____

3. In the depths of winter, a brutal snowstorm traps the residents of a remote mountain resort town with a Yeti-like creature that starts hunting them for sport.

_____

_____

_____

_____

_____

. To prove their devotion to a dark deity, cult members embark on a ree of brutal human sacrifices—until the deity demands their own kin as yment.

_____

_____

_____

_____

_____

85. Nick Nottingham had done plenty of dreamwork before, but never had he been stalked by something as persistent and disarming as the man with the ram's head.

_____

_____

_____

_____

_____

86. She never slept. Whether she was in my bedroom or my bathroom or waiting in the hallway, the woman who haunted my childhood was always alert and always looking to eat my years.

_____

_____

_____

_____

87. The cruise ship entered the mists and the crew yelled at the guests to to their cabins, only the captain knowing that the beasts would take who they wanted, whether there were doors or not.

_____

_____

_____

_____

88. The ghosts of famous authors gather to inspire a young blind boy wr story that will save humanity.

_____

_____

_____

_____

89. A struggling artist paints a series of eerie portraits while high on substances, only to find that each subject suffers a gruesome fate shortly after their likeness is captured on canvas.

_____

_____

_____

_____

_____

90. In the aftermath of a devastating earthquake, the survivors must navigate their way through a labyrinth of underground tunnels teeming with grotesque creatures hungry for human flesh.

_____

_____

_____

_____

_____

91. When Maria loses her daughter to cancer, she turns to the occult arts to bring her daughter back, accidentally summoning something wicked craving a human vessel.

_____

_____

_____

_____

_____

92. She knew why the demon had brought her there—her mother. And as her mother's daughter, she was determined to send the demon up to heaven, to burn in God's light forever.

_____

_____

_____

_____

_____

93. In the depths of a deserted diamond mine, long-forgotten horrors awaken when a group of enterprising explorers open a sealed door.

_____

_____

_____

_____

_____

94. The dollhouse wasn't there before. And when Amelia opened it up, she saw it mirrored her own home... except for lurking things in the most shadowed corners of the miniature house.

_____

_____

_____

_____

_____

95. A psychic detective is called in to help solve a series of grisly murders plaguing a city, only to discover that the killer is the "Grim Maw", a supernatural entity from her own haunted past.

_____

_____

_____

_____

_____

96. A renowned ghost hunter who lost her parents as a child faces her greatest challenge yet when she uncovers evidence of an ancient curse that threatens to consume the rest of her family.

_____

_____

_____

_____

_____

97. When the choice was between dying and becoming a servant of the undead, it got real easy to make a decision.

---

98. We moved through the jungle, sweat in our eyes and down our backs. Everyone wanted to stop, but we'd already seen what the centipedes could do and didn't want to be next.

---

99. A talented sculptor becomes obsessed with creating lifelike statues but soon realizes that her creations are taking on a life of their own.

---

100. When an antique mirror that reveals sinister reflections of its observers' darkest secrets and desires is put on display at a local museum, a city is slowly consumed by madness.

---

101. NewU, a new virtual reality game, becomes horrifyingly real as players find themselves unable to escape the nightmarish world they've entered.

_____
_____
_____
_____
_____

102. In a small, isolated village, the townsfolk gather every year to perform a ritual to keep a malevolent vampiric force at bay. But this year, with the blood well empty, there is no stopping the carnage.

_____
_____
_____
_____
_____

103. We were all going to die in this airport, but that's the way it had to be i the Grendel was to be contained.

_____
_____
_____
_____
_____

104. Not all vampires deserved to die. But Vincent thought they should all staked and turned to ash anyway.

_____
_____
_____
_____
_____

105. Never look in a mirror for more than a minute. That's how he finds you.

---

106. The peaceful town of Greenwich is turned upside down when a sexually transmitted disease starts turning people into bloodthirsty ghouls.

---

07. After being attacked by a werewolf, a detective discovers that the creature is actually an old friend—and now they must work together to bring down the secret organization responsible for the transformation.

---

8. You think you know what pain feels like, but believe you me, there is no pain like realizing you are but a bug to something meaner and superior to yourself.

ROMANCE WRITING PROMPTS

"If you don't go after what you want, you'll never have it. If you don't ask, the answer is always no. If you don't step forward, you're always in the same place."

Nora Roberts

1. In Victorian London, a sweets shop owner and a brooding playwright find themselves drawn together by a plot to drive attendance to the playwright's latest performance.

_____

_____

_____

_____

_____

2. At an annual masquerade ball in Chicago, two strangers share an unforgettable waltz that leaves them both questioning whether it was just enchantment or if they somehow knew each other from a past life.

_____

_____

_____

_____

_____

3. Write about two rival stage magicians who find themselves handcuffed together during performance practice and must work as one to escape not only their predicament while their attraction grows.

_____

_____

_____

_____

_____

4. As he languidly sketched her nude form during their private art lessons, fledgling painter Raphael knew he'd eventually have to tell his gorgeous muse Elizabeth that no one would buy his works.

_____

_____

_____

_____

_____

5. The moment her lips touched the forbidden fruit, Eve found herself in a sinfully passionate embrace with Adam that would change the course of human history—again.

_____

_____

_____

_____

_____

6. In the distant future, when holographic partners are the norm, a lonely programmer named Isabelle creates the perfect digital companion in the form of charming machine-generated poet Oliver—only to discover that he actually become sentient and is longing to be human.

_____

_____

_____

_____

_____

7. As they lay tangled in each other's arms after a passionate rendezvous in the moonlit forest, psychic medium Celeste realized she had broken her own cardinal rule by falling in love with the spirit of charming outlaw, James.

_____

_____

_____

_____

_____

8. At midnight on New Year's Eve, heartbroken bar owner Jack found himself sharing an unexpected kiss with notorious flirt and party planner Sophie—with neither realizing that they had just sealed a year-long bet to make each other fall in love.

_____

_____

_____

_____

_____

9. Melissa hadn't meant to fall for her brother-in-law, but love never gave a damn about what it did to who and when it did it.

_____

_____

_____

_____

10. Write about two lovers who communicate solely through letters exchanged by carrier pigeon, their identities remaining unknown to each other until they must meet to save their small town from being bought out by a mining corporation.

_____

_____

_____

_____

1. After being assigned as personal bodyguard to Hollywood's hottest actor Benjamin Steele, former military officer Jenna must protect him from danger while resisting their sizzling chemistry.

_____

_____

_____

_____

. Under the bright lights of Broadway, two young actors find their dreams intertwined as they pursue both stardom and love on the stage. But only one of them can make it big, forcing them to choose who will succeed and who will give up their burgeoning fame.

_____

_____

_____

_____

13. A love potion goes awry at a magical boarding school, causing students and teachers alike to fall head-over-heels for the wrong people and creating chaos that two young wizards who hate each other must resolve, realizing through their actions that they actually care for one another.

14. She couldn't speak his name—not now, after he'd broken her heart aga

15. When renowned therapist Dr. Clara Reid is assigned to counsel notorious playboy Jake Hamilton after his latest scandal, she finds herself unable to resist his constant flirtations.

16. A heartbroken florist finds solace and inspiration in the tender word an anonymous poet who leaves handwritten verses among her flowers e: morning, until one day the notes stop coming.

17. While exploring the mystical ruins of an ancient castle, two historians uncover secrets that are hundreds of years old that ignite a shared passion while also drawing a mercenary group who wish to use the secrets to make their employer rich.

_____

_____

_____

_____

_____

18. After being hired as a personal assistant to eccentric millionaire Xavier, ambitious young administrative assistant Zoe finds herself drawn towards Xavier's down-to-earth sister.

_____

_____

_____

_____

_____

19. When two single parents meet at their children's soccer game, they're surprised to find that their attraction for one another is enough to make them forget their lost spouses.

_____

_____

_____

_____

_____

20. As they raced through the city streets on his motorcycle, adrenaline pumping through their veins, bad boy Jax challenged Mia to let go of his hips and trust him to keep her safe on her bike.

_____

_____

_____

_____

21. After a one-night stand leaves billionaire CEO Jeremy Holden with amnesia, he relies on free-spirited artist Karla Dupree to help him recover his memories—leading him down a path of shame at how he earned his riches and a chance for redemption.

_____

_____

_____

_____

_____

22. The hardest thing I ever did was admitting to myself how much I cared about you. It meant I could no longer give into my depression or my anger or my sense that nothing in this world was meant to work out. I wish I could say I hate you for making me feel that way, but I could never hate you.

_____

_____

_____

_____

_____

23. When a broken-hearted woman takes refuge in a remote lighthouse, she never expects to find solace and healing in the arms of its rugged keeper who has said to be cold and uncaring.

_____

_____

_____

_____

_____

24. When an esteemed pianist loses her ability to play, she finds healing and love in the arms of a humble piano tuner who helps her rediscover her passion for music, convincing her to give up her aspirations for fame and focus on playing for people who can't afford fancy, expensive concerts.

_____

_____

_____

_____

25. After nearly drowning during an intense storm at sea, shipwreck survivor Eliza washes ashore on a deserted island and finds herself falling for the island's mysterious sole inhabitant, Tristan. But is Tristan truly as wonderful and caring as he seems?

_____

_____

_____

_____

_____

26. When literary professor Olivia discovers that her favorite author is actually her reclusive neighbor, she embarks on a quest to learn more about the enigmatic man behind the words, risking her tenured position as she forgoes her duties as a professor.

_____

_____

_____

_____

_____

27. Even though everyone said the sparks had been flying between Mitchell and Denise all night, Denise's heart belonged to another.

_____

_____

_____

_____

_____

28. After hiring a male escort to pose as her boyfriend to make her ex jealous, advertising executive Vivian finds herself falling for him as she explores her deepest desires with him while inviting him to open up to her in a way he's never done before.

_____

_____

_____

_____

29. I want to love you for who you are," she said. "But most of all, I want to be loved for who I am.

_____
_____
_____
_____
_____

30. After being jilted at the altar, heartbroken Emily embarks on her honeymoon in Bali alone, unaware that she's about to meet the love of her life.

_____
_____
_____
_____
_____

31. Trapped together in a sweltering elevator for hours, Olivia had to finally admit that handsome handyman Max made her feel unlike anyone at her law firm did.

_____
_____
_____
_____
_____

32. When the fringe marine biologist Dr. Amelia Rivers discovers a rare and elusive mermaid named Lorelei, she finds herself torn between her duty to science and a blossoming romance that could change everything about her life.

_____
_____
_____
_____

33. Cassidy always knew she would find love where she'd first lost it.

---

34. He waited in the rain for her, letting his suit get ruined and his shoes get soaked. But she only watched him through the window, afraid of what he'd say when he saw her true face.

---

5. In a mystical forest where desire takes shape as magical creatures called stlings, sheltered princess Aurora encounters a dashing rogue named iden while she's in the form of a hare, wondering how she'll ever meet him gain outside of the enchanted woods.

. In a wondrous world where people can see the color of their soulmate's ra, a colorblind artist finds love after creating a stunning work for public splay.

---

37. A free-spirited artist and a straight-laced architect are thrown together when they're forced to share studio space, but their clashing personalities soon give way to electric attraction that they'll need to use to keep their studio space from being bought out by a greedy real estate developer.

_____
_____
_____
_____
_____

38. A down-on-her-luck romance novelist suddenly finds herself living ou the passionate love stories she's only written about when she meets her mu a man exactly like her male leads who hates everything she's ever written.

_____
_____
_____
_____
_____

39. On a solo trip around the world, travel blogger Sophie falls head over heels for her charming tour guide Alejandro while exploring the ruins of Machu Picchu, but the two are soon separated during a freak earthquake

_____
_____
_____
_____
_____

40. In the heat of battle during a medieval jousting tournament, tall and stately Lady Eleanor found herself inexplicably drawn to her opponent— brooding Sir William.

_____
_____
_____
_____
_____

41. I knew her before I became the man I am today. That's why she only sees the boy who made all those mistakes.

_____

_____

_____

_____

_____

42. Jerome had went back to Atlanta one last time to pay his debts, never expecting to stay with the love of his life.

_____

_____

_____

_____

43. When overworked Director of Marketing Sarah takes an impromptu vacation to Hawaii, she is swept off her feet by charming surf instructor Kai and discovers that sometimes, paradise is more than just a place—it's a state of mind.

_____

_____

_____

_____

44. Imagine your favorite romance story, television show, or movie, but imagine it ending with the leads not getting together. What happened?

_____

_____

_____

_____

45. The elevator doors closed as Tess looked at Terry for the last time.

_____

_____

_____

_____

_____

46. People always said "the heart wants what the heart wants", but those people had never met that jerk Lance.

_____

_____

_____

_____

_____

47. During an unlikely and unexpected encounter at a luxurious hot spring resort in Iceland, heartbroken Fiona finds herself drawn to the grumpy, introverted Magnus as they wind up the last two guests in the beautiful geothermal pools.

_____

_____

_____

_____

_____

48. In a quaint French village, two rivals in the annual baking competition find that their secret ingredient is not just sugar and spice, but an undenia chemistry and desire to best one another.

_____

_____

_____

_____

_____

49. When world-famous chocolatier Adrian receives an anonymous love letter crafted from edible chocolate ink, he becomes obsessed with finding the secret admirer behind this culinary masterpiece, as obsessed with them as he is jealous of their talents.

---

50. As the train rattled through the night, Cassie found herself locked in a heated tryst with Lucien, aka Mr. Tall, Pale, and Handsome, unaware of his true intentions.

---

51. In a world where people wear their hearts on their sleeves—literally—a young woman with a broken heart embarks on a journey to mend it with the help of a childhood friend who always had a crush on her.

---

52. On the eve of the summer solstice, two distant neighbors are inexplicably drawn together at a magical midsummer festival, where they dance and dream under the moonlit sky; in the morning, one of them is gone, leaving the other to search the surrounding towns for them.

---

53. As a talented ghostwriter pens the memoir of a mysterious billionaire, she finds herself drawn into his hidden world and captivated by his enigmatic charm.

_____

_____

_____

_____

_____

54. After surviving a near-death experience, successful businesswoman Sadie begins receiving love letters from an unknown admirer in the afterlife leading her on an unexpected journey of self-discovery and passion.

_____

_____

_____

_____

_____

55. A sleepwalking woman embarks on nightly adventures guided by her subconscious desires, eventually leading her into the arms of a charming insomniac neighbor who joins her on these nocturnal escapades, afraid to admit his role in her sleepwalking in the light of day.

_____

_____

_____

_____

_____

56. When struggling actress Lucy lands the role of Juliet in a modern adaptation of Shakespeare's classic tale, she finds herself falling for her Romeo—played by a woman—both on stage and off.

_____

_____

_____

_____

57. When paranormal investigator Serena goes undercover at an exclusive vampire nightclub, she finds herself drawn into a dangerous affair with its vampiric, seductive owner, Sebastian.

_____
_____
_____
_____
_____

58. At an exclusive ski resort, adrenaline junkie and snowboarding instructor Alex unexpectedly finds love with high-strung executive Catherine as he teaches her to let go of her uptight ways.

_____
_____
_____
_____
_____

59. As she stepped from behind the curtain onto the burlesque stage for the first time, undercover detective Emma couldn't have anticipated that she would fall for notorious crime boss Vinny Cement Shoes.

_____
_____
_____
_____
_____

. Describe your ideal first date only using your non-sight senses of touch, smell, hearing, and taste.

_____
_____
_____
_____
_____

61. Even though he was dead, she was determined to keep their love alive.

_____
_____
_____
_____
_____

62. During a passionate tango lesson, a reserved scientist learns to embrac her sensual side and unexpectedly falls for her enigmatic dance partner— who happens to be her ex-husband's best friend.

_____
_____
_____
_____

63. After accidentally switching bodies with her sworn enemy, uptight lawyer Camilla must navigate the complexities of their newfound life as a street performer and her newfound attraction to her borrowed body whi struggling to reverse the spell cast upon them.

_____
_____
_____
_____

64. It was their first Christmas together, their secret love eager to be kno

_____
_____
_____
_____

65. During Prohibition-era New Orleans, speakeasy owner Desmond finds himself swept up in a whirlwind romance with vivacious jazz singer Lila as they navigate a lurking danger that threatens all of New Orleans.

_____

_____

_____

_____

_____

66. As they raced through the streets of Paris after their heist gone awry, cat burglar Bella found herself furious with and falling for her square-jawed partner in crime, Edgar.

_____

_____

_____

_____

_____

67. As Roslyn looked over the patrons seated at the hotel bar, she had no idea one of them would be her future husband—in fifteen years.

_____

_____

_____

_____

_____

68. After finding a mysterious letter hidden in an old book, a shy librarian embarks on a quest to reunite the star-crossed lovers mentioned in the letter—only to discover that she is one of them.

_____

_____

_____

_____

69. The moment their hands accidentally brushed against each other in the dimly lit library, sparks ignited between Professor Victoria Sinclair and young archeologist James Harrington, setting off a passionate affair that would challenge the very foundations of their careers.

_____

_____

_____

_____

_____

70. While attending separate destination weddings in picturesque Tuscany, two lonely guests realize they may have found the love they're seeking in each other, even though both of them are in relationships already.

_____

_____

_____

_____

_____

71. The worst part about heartbreak wasn't the big, bombastic ending of a deep and meaningful relationship, it was the phantom desire that never seemed to wane.

_____

_____

_____

_____

_____

72. In the steamy depths of a 1940s New York jazz club, talented trumpeter Damien found himself captivated by the soulful voice of charming singer Lola.

_____

_____

_____

_____

_____

73. Write from the perspective of a sentient AI who falls in love with its human creator and tries to win their affection through subtle acts of kindness and support, only to struggle to understand what it means to be human.

_____

_____

_____

_____

_____

74. After discovering the diary of an ancestor from centuries ago, a woman realizes her own love story mirrors that of her long-lost relative, and seeks guidance from the past to navigate her present relationship with hair-raising results.

_____

_____

_____

_____

_____

75. Write about a couple who find themselves trapped in an endless loop of their first date, forced to confront their fears and insecurities until they decide whether or not they want to remain together.

_____

_____

_____

_____

_____

76. On her 30th birthday, commitment-phobic Lila wakes up in a parallel universe where she's already married to her longtime boyfriend—will this glimpse of happily ever after change her mind or will she decide she needs more?

_____

_____

_____

_____

77. Struggling fashion designer Bella finds herself drawn into an illicit romance with her boss's husband after he becomes her secret benefactor.

_____

_____

_____

_____

_____

78. Write about a magical bookstore where patrons can enter the worlds of their favorite novels, leading one woman to find unexpected love in the pages of a classic romance written by her great aunt.

_____

_____

_____

_____

_____

79. When her car broke down in the middle of a stormy night, stranded city girl Emma sought shelter at a nearby farmhouse—only to find herself tangled up in an illicit affair with a brusque farmhand named Luke.

_____

_____

_____

_____

_____

80. Write from the perspective of a lovestruck ghost who must solve their own murder mystery to be reunited with their soulmate in the afterlife.

_____

_____

_____

_____

_____

81. My mother told me never to fall in love, but I swore I'd never be as miserable as she was.

_____
_____
_____
_____
_____

82. After finding an old map hidden in the attic, adventurous hot-and-cold couple Emily and Ben embark on a treasure hunt for lost pirate gold. But soon they'll discover they aren't the only ones searching for the treasure.

_____
_____
_____
_____
_____

83. The second their eyes met across the crowded lobby of the luxurious desert resort, exotic dancer Layla knew she had found her match.

_____
_____
_____
_____
_____

84. Decades from now, when people are matched through a DNA compatibility test, free-spirited dancer Lily discovers her perfect match is none other than the cold-hearted CEO of the company behind the test, Alistair King.

_____
_____
_____
_____

85. After discovering a hidden room filled with erotic paintings in her inherited mansion, shy heiress Lisandra must confront her own desires as she unravels the scandalous past of her ancestors and finds herself drawn to the enigmatic curator assisting her research.

_____

_____

_____

_____

_____

86. Write about who your ideal partner would be without mentioning any their physical characteristics.

_____

_____

_____

_____

87. An aspiring musician meets her muse when she stumbles upon an old jazz club, but will they be able to navigate their feelings when she learns the club is soon going to be shut down?

_____

_____

_____

_____

_____

88. Two estranged childhood friends reunite at a high school reunion only to discover that they now live in neighboring apartments, leading them to rekindle old feelings.

_____

_____

_____

_____

89. When two spies from opposing government organizations are assigned to infiltrate each other's ranks, they find themselves trapped in a dangerous game of trust and betrayal while falling in love, unsure if either's love is real or simply part of their deception.

_____

_____

_____

_____

_____

90. When a world-renowned chef and a talented food critic unknowingly cross paths at a culinary retreat, their shared passion for flavors ignites an unexpected romance.

_____

_____

_____

_____

_____

91. At a bustling international airport, two delayed travelers bond over shared heartaches while waiting out an endless layover, questioning if they should both change their travel plans and go somewhere else together.

_____

_____

_____

_____

_____

92. n an underwater city inhabited by merpeople, two ex-lovers find hemselves tangled in a forbidden, rekindled romance that could put their ntire kingdom at risk.

_____

_____

_____

_____

93. During their impromptu duet at an open-mic night, struggling musician Charlie became entranced by sultry singer Delilah's voice, finding a reason to play his songs once more.

_____

_____

_____

_____

_____

94. When an amateur gardener unearths a magical flower that blooms only when true love is near, she must navigate the quirky characters of her small town to find its intended recipients, not realizing that her quest will bring her towards her own love as well.

_____

_____

_____

_____

_____

95. After being magically transported back in time to ancient Rome, modern-day archaeologist and Latin scholar Diana must navigate the dangerous politics of the era while falling for gladiator Titus.

_____

_____

_____

_____

_____

96. Las Vegas wasn't where you went to fall in true love, yet there Peter and Miranda were, the only sober people in the whole crowd, afraid that after tonight the magic would wear off.

_____

_____

_____

_____

97. As their families feud over control of an esteemed vineyard, two passionate winemakers must keep their blossoming love secret to protect their shared dream of creating the perfect vintage that neither family could ever truly own.

_____

_____

_____

_____

_____

98. A time-traveling historian accidentally falls in love with a dashing pirate captain from the 18th century, forcing her to make an impossible choice between her life in the present and the allure of adventure on the high seas.

_____

_____

_____

_____

_____

99. As the last descendant of the legendary Queen Cleopatra, modern-day archaeologist Aida seeks to uncover her family's hidden history, only to discover her ancestor was not who she thought.

_____

_____

_____

_____

_____

100. Write about your own first experience with love, imagining how things might have gone differently.

_____

_____

_____

_____

101. The day you told me you loved me was the day I decided to live my life to its fullest.

_____

_____

_____

_____

_____

102. When renowned heart surgeon Dr. Amelia Grey receives an anonymous bouquet of flowers with a cryptic message from someone claiming to be a past patient, she becomes obsessed with uncovering the identity of her secret admirer despite the ethical dilemma in doing so.

_____

_____

_____

_____

_____

103. Write about a young woman and romance novelist who inherits her grandmother's antique locket, only to discover it contains the key to unlocking a long-lost love story.

_____

_____

_____

_____

_____

104. She was in my dreams, every night, even though we'd never said a word to each other.

_____

_____

_____

_____

_____

105. In a land where pheromones determine one's perfect match, rebellious perfumer Elise creates a fragrance that allows her to disguise her true scent—until she encounters alluring chemist Nicholas who sees through her deception and exposes her deepest desires.

_____

_____

_____

_____

_____

106. In a fantastic world where true love depends on deciphering a cryptic code sent by Cupid himself, computer hacker Eva sets out to crack the code and accidentally falls for her rival programmer, Alexei.

_____

_____

_____

_____

_____

107. While exploring the steamy jungles of Borneo in search of a rare orchid, botanist Melissa found the rarest flower of all in her travelling companion, Nicholas.

_____

_____

_____

_____

108. You said that I was the key to your heart, but what if I don't want to be the key? What if I want to be the lock for someone else to open?

_____

_____

_____

_____

Thank You!

The Mayday writing team sincerely hopes you enjoyed this book and found it to be another antidote to your writer's block woes. If you did enjoy it, we encourage you to leave a review on Amazon to clue others in and to help another writer build productive, creative habits.

Until next time,
The Mayday Writing Collective

Also by the Mayday Writing Collective:

The Original Genre Writers Idea Book

r those of you who haven't seen the original Genre Writer's Book, be sure to eck out these 540 completely unique story ideas and writing prompts across e different genres! Available on Amazon for Kindle, Kindle Unlimited and a Paperback.

Made in the USA
Las Vegas, NV
21 December 2023

83352672R00089